In the stirring Silence

Reflections on life

Dr. Daisy Dharmaraj

BookLeaf Publishing

India | USA | UK

Dedication

This book is dedicated to the women and men who have stood resilient against inequalities, divisions and adversities – be it due to gender, race, poverty, patriarchy or HIV/AIDS. I also dedicate this work to my friends and family, whose affection and encouragement have been my unwavering strength. May their struggles begin to cease, and may they find equity and equality in due time.

Acknowledgements

Writing this book has been an enriching journey shaped by my experiences in Sri Lanka and India. I am deeply grateful to the many individuals who have influenced my life – each one contributing to my values, career and personal growth. To those whose resilience has inspired me, and to my family and friends for their unwavering support, I extend my heartfelt thanks.

Above all, I thank God for being my guide and source of strength

Preface

My early years were overshadowed by the dangers of civil war. Decades of involvement with and exposure to diverse people and cultures have greatly enriched my understanding, while the challenges along this journey have strengthened me. I have drawn profound lessons from vulnerable communities, including those affected by caste, gender, poverty, HIV/AIDS and disabilities.

These poems are born from cherished memories, surprising joys, moments of reflection and deep insights. If even one poem resonates with readers, this endeavour will be truly worthwhile.

Betrayal

She stood clutching the blood report,
Her face etched with anguish, fear and pain.
At seventeen, young and beautiful, full of
dreams,
She married her sweetheart.

Life was blissful – a daughter to cherish,
His business thriving as an autorickshaw
driver
In a town shadowed by a red-light district,
Where brothels stood amidst the auto
industry.

Now, she is pregnant again,
Yet the joy was drowned in a wave of anguish.

Bursting into the clinic, sad and furious,
Her cries broke into uncontrollable sobs.

The truth was undeniable–
She was HIV-positive.
Dreams shattered, her future a question mark.
What of her daughter?
What of the baby she carried?

Her agony was unbearable.
Her beloved, the one she trusted most,
Had betrayed her in the cruellest way.
How could he? Didn't he care?

He leaves her to bear the weight–
Her life, her children's lives,
Forever scarred by his deceit.
He knew... yet he stayed silent,
Betraying the trust of their love,
Not protecting her from being infected.

A love once pure, now tainted,
By his selfish choice to conceal.
The joy they built together–
Now overshadowed by anguish and loss.

The abandoned slipper

The lone slipper on the roadside,
Tells myriad of stories

Once it adorned a foot–
A pillion rider's or the rider's own?
Someone crossing in haste?
A person dragged unwillingly?

A woman fleeing a tyrant?
A drunkard stumbling along?
An elder who lost their way?
A traveller, struggling through the night?

A child cradled in someone's arms?
A rich man, indifferent?
A poor woman who could not afford another?
A vendor on the scorching, tarry road?

On the sidewalk, it lies–
Forsaken, forgotten,
Lost to the world.
The abandoned slipper

Life's Drama: The Giver is the Receiver

Walking down the lonely, narrow road to the clinic,
I felt the thorns prick my saree,
Twisting and turning, yet finding no escape.
Despair crept in; I couldn't even cry out.
Seeing my distress, a field worker hurried over,
Carefully cleared away the thorns, setting me free
Relief washed over me as I sighed in gratitude,
Offering a quiet thanks before walking away,

Weeks later, during a quiet shift at the clinic,
A sudden commotion broke the stillness outside.
A man, electrocuted, was brought into the casualty
His body limp; his pulse and heart rate undetectable.

For the first time as a medico, hesitation
gripped me.
I injected adrenaline directly into his chest.
I held my breath, the seconds stretched
endless
Until it happened. A pulse.

His heartbeat returned; nothing short of a
miracle.
Call it skill or luck, or perhaps both

The reason I write this
Is to share an uncanny coincidence:
The man I saved that night
Was the one who saved me from the thorns.

What would you call this...
A circle complete?

Where will Banu go

A dignified elder woman walked in,
A broad, captivating smile on her face.
Little did I know, behind that smile,
Lay a mother's sorrow, hidden away.

Her adult daughter followed, confused,
Meeting my eyes, unsure, troubled.
Banu, a beauty, intellectually challenged,
Repeating words, meaninglessly echoing.

Then I saw her father, neat and refined,
A friendly smile, a face so pleasant.
Once, their shop had thrived,
Comfortable life, surrounded by friends.

Banu loves to dance, sings with her father,
A simple joy, though life's been cruel.
Mother and daughter, both severely diabetic,
Banu epileptic too – an added struggle.

The mother, bright and eager, wins every
competition.

She is the life of the party, always radiating
joy.
The father's romantic songs with deep feeling,
Evokes memories in all who listen.

Trusting, caring, with hearts so pure,
Her father deceived in trade and business,
Now reliant on charity, as life grows dim.
Trampled by society that cares so little

Now no visitors come, relatives stay away,
Each day is a battle – physical, emotional.
Their hopes shattered, their pain runs deep.
What does the future hold? Their sad eyes
weep.

A leaking roof, most often an empty kitchen,
Medicine bottles empty, no money to buy.
As age advances, both need care,
With an adult daughter needing constant
watch.

When disease and age steal their strength and
life?

Where will Banu go, with none by her side???

Lest you forget

Never forget those moments of support–
A caring look from a stranger,
An understanding smile,
A voice that spoke for you.
Believed in you, even when you were wrong.
The one who paid your dues,
Bought you a notebook, a dress when in need,

Raised you up when you were down,
Hugged you when distressed,
Sheltered you when cast out
Held your hands as you crossed over the
storms

Patiently listened when you reviled in anger,
Offered advice or reprimanded when needed,
A parent who loved you unconditionally
Your gurus who showed you the way
For it's them who shaped the real YOU,
Helping you survive in this mad, mad world–
As I often remind myself,
Having received all of this.

Humbled by the Mighty Himalayas

It was a small plane,
Sixteen of us, gliding through the sky,
My teenage daughter and I, hearts racing with
awe,
Flying over the Himalayas – Earth's towering
giants.

Who could have imagined this moment?
Strapped in our orange safety suits,
The engine roared, and we ascended,
The ethereal blue-black peaks unfolding
below,

Soaring higher and higher into the heavens.
The sheer scale, the raw power of these
mountains,
Left us breathless, humbled by their grandeur.
We gazed in wide-eyed wonder,
Absorbing the sight as clouds rushed by,
Peaks, glaciers shimmering in the sunlight.
At times, enveloped entirely in white,

Suspended in the heart of the clouds,
As if the world had paused around us.
Where sorrow fades and time stands still,
Timeless, eternal, forever pure.

Himalayas–

you have sheltered sages,
Offering wisdom profound.
You have also claimed countless seekers,
Those who dared your heights.

Human lives fade, yet you would remain–
Majestic, untouched, preserved, eternal.
A sanctuary for the soul,
Reflecting the splendour of your maker.

An Ode to the 69ers

Diverse backgrounds, religions, ages and
personas.
We grew up together – some brisk, some slow.
Nerds, musicians, singers, leaders, athletes,
artists,
Speakers, dreamers, romantics and skeptics.
Religious, cynical; shy, spunky; bold, not so
bold.
A few from across the seas,
Others from different corners of India.

Ragging, college bus rides, classes, clinicals,
get-togethers, exams,
Choirs, dramas, games, festivals, carols. Class
trips, climbing hills alone or in company,

Visits to cinemas and Buhari's in Chennai.
Hostel mess, Y-cutlets, corner shop, Bagayam
tea stalls and other haunts.

We stood by each other in heartaches and
sorrows,
Jumped to the moon and back for each
other's joys.
Helped each other with studies,
Cried together in our failures.
Teased when love blossomed, wept when
hearts broke,
Rose in protest when injustice struck,
Mourned deeply when a friend passed away.
As basic doctors, we parted–
Emerging as specialists, some renowned,

Taking risks, facing challenges, sacrificing
comforts,
Working tirelessly with zeal and care. It was a
golden period.
Now in the phase of slowing down–

Some grey, some occasionally grey, Some
bearded or moustached, some not. Wrinkled
– some well concealed,
With ailments, we barely bother to count.

A few have passed on, leaving us memories to
cherish
Yet, we remain connected, threads of
friendship unbroken–
Bound by laughter, tears and shared dreams
of youth.
In this circle of life, we hold each other still,

Golden years engraved forever in our hearts.
Three cheers to the Silver and Blue

Yes... I can

A girl in class eleven,
Yes, quite far I've come!
I've seen the world from the edges,
But I'm ready now to merge!

 I was born with my eyes set not so right,
And people stared, so horrified!
They covered their kids' eyes too,
Afraid they'd get scared and cry.

I felt sad and wished it would all disappear.
'Why me'? I asked as I looked at my face.
Yet, my parents and therapists loved me,
Gave me strength to move on

We couldn't afford the surgery,
But hope began to shine–
Some kind hearts stepped in,
I could see a ray of hope

I had the surgery, long and arduous,
Recovery was not easy– I was
scared, rebellious and I wept,
But soon, I started to see my altered face!

Slowly, I began to change,
It took some time, but it was worth the wait.
Now, I look in the mirror,
And I feel like I'm nearly like the others.

Still am conscious and quiet
My arms need mending too
I study hard as it will be my strength
I'm an independent girl and I stand tall.

I smile at the moon and stars so bright,
I smell the sweet flowers, I feel the peace.
With my newfound confidence,
I sure can take on the world

The Mystery of the
Missing Boarding Card

The flight attendant called,
'Boarding cards, please, hold them tight!
There's a strict inspection coming,
So make sure they're in sight'!

My heart did a flip,
I searched all around,
Not in my pouch, not in my passport,
Where could it be?

In Kenya, a strange new land
I'll have to face this somehow.
I stood up, feeling unsure,
Took a last look at my seat, for sure.

My glance fell on the window,
Right next to my seat,
And there it was, stuck on the glass
My boarding card winking at me.

How on earth did it get there?
I'll never know, it's a mystery fair.
But I could smile; a sigh of relief,
I guess Nairobi's got a bit of magic, don't you
think?

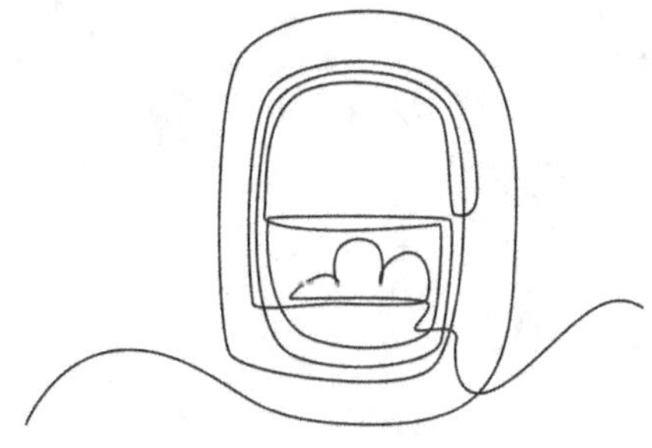

Rejected people

A carefree, happy little girl,
Cherished, pampered, petted.
At school, the teachers adored her–
Well-behaved, well-dressed, smart.
She sang sweetly, acted in plays,

She shone in every way.
She and her friends began piano lessons.
The first day was full of joy,
But the next, she was stopped at the gate.
The tutor said, 'You cannot learn here
anymore'.

Crestfallen, she turned away.
It was her first taste of rejection and bias–

A concept she couldn't even fathom.
She grew up, entered university,
Fell in love with a kind young man,
Love succumbed to hell's fury from his family
Well, she was of a lower caste.

Her education, compassion, her looks–
None of this mattered.
And for women in poverty, it's far worse,
While the privileged have shields of
protection.

Caste raises its ugly head,
In every town and village of the land,
Beneath layers of smiles and benevolence–
A non-negotiable factor, that is sure.
The laws of the land cannot do justice.

Discrimination reigns supreme.
A casteless society? What a bitter dream...!

A Silent Sacrifice

In a town in Guntur district,
She lived with her father, a labourer.
Her mother died when she was small,
Her father, her whole world.

Like many in the slum,
She dropped out of school,
Too many chores in her tiny abode–
Cooking, washing, collecting water,
Giggles, kajal on her eyes,
Flowers in her hair, red lipstick on her lips.

One day, her father fell ill,
Fever, stomach pain, vomiting.
She rushed him to the hospital,
Only to hear it was advanced appendicitis.
The operation cost seven thousand rupees,
A sum too large for her world.

No gold to pawn,
No sarees to sell,
No way to get the money.
The auto driver, seeing her distress, said,
'If you sleep with a man for an hour,
The money will be yours'.

She sobbed, knowing she was her father's only
hope,
Her dreams of a wedding, a future, slipping
away.
With fear and despair in her eyes,
She walked with him to the lodge,

From then on, the sharks never left her,
Her body was now her means to survive.
The strength of her soul ebbed away,
Her feelings turned to stone.

Her story, like so many others,
Heart-wrenching and silent,
Caught in poverty and violence–
She sold her soul to buy him breath,
A daughter's love, an immeasurable sacrifice.

Seeds of Wonder, Seeds of Control

The mustard seed becomes a shrub,
Tiny yellow flowers blooming bright.
A fiery chilli seed sprouts tender green,
Drooping white flowers give way to spice.
From where does the burning flavour arise?

The black papaya seeds birth small trees,
Bearing fruits, green to yellow to red–
When did their sweetness and colours appear?

A woman plants them in a modest tray,
Tending and watering with loving care.
Her heart swells when tiny sprouts emerge,
Each a miracle of life unseen.
For when I crush the seed, I find no spark,
Yet within it hides the mystery of creation.
Soil, water and sunlight weave their magic,
Unfolding the eternal wonder of growth.
Seeds – the timeless gift of nature,
Free for all to sow, share and cherish.

But greed has claimed what once was free.
The rich now steal from nature's bounty,
Tinkering with life, altering the seed,
To own its essence, its fruit, its power.
'To feed the millions', they proclaim,
Yet public wealth becomes private gain.

Modified seeds – resistant, controlled,
Patents lock their secrets away.
Small farmers enslaved to soaring costs,
Sustainable, healthy food grows rare.

The soil, the earth, poisoned by greed,
A sacred trust violated, betrayed.
Corporate hands, playing God,
Own the life that was once nature's gift.

The seeds – now symbols of power, not life,
Leave nations hungry, and justice denied.

A legacy

Today, I remember with reverence and grace,
Your 129th birthday, in this cherished space.
I see your smile, hear your voice call my
name,
In bright whites, you stood; a beacon, a flame.

A man of brilliance, a builder par excellence,
Hospitals, lighthouses, your work supreme.
Jaffna's Town Hall, a marvel of pride,
A public figure respected far and wide.

At home, your presence – a powerful storm,
Anger tempered with care, love in its form.
But we didn't see it, as it wasn't displayed,
In the way we expected or the way we prayed.
To the needy you gave, with hands open wide,
Helping families numerous, with your care

You challenged caste, a warrior for right,
Fighting injustice with unyielding might.
Amidst attempts to annihilate you and your quest
Life's burdens were heavy, the journey was long,
Yet through it all, your resolve stayed strong.
The day came too soon when you slipped away,
We held your hand as you faded that day.

Twas through stories unearthed by an angel's mission,
I learned later the depth of your fight, your unrest.
A champion for justice, a voice for the weak,
You stood for humanity, bold and unique.

Thank you, Papa, for all that you gave,
For paving paths so others could be free.
Your legacy lingers, a guiding light true,
I'm ever proud to be your daughter.

God in Shadows and Storms

In Sri Lanka's turmoil, where fear took its
hold,
Terror and uncertainty, stories untold.
Kamala's people, a minority, caught in the
strife,
Many lost all – belongings, numerous lives.
Through riots and struggles, in '58 and '77,
Poverty and fear, no peace to be given.
Though the government sought to restore the
calm,
Terror reigned, and hearts knew no balm.

One dark day, she travelled to the office with
a friend,
As dusk fell, she chose to return home alone.
The rain poured down, and streets grew dim,
She prayed for protection, afraid but hopeful.
She took determined steps, towards her house
on the hill,
The world around her felt cold as stone.
Few people lingered, no women in sight,

She felt the weight of the darkened night.

Twas then that she sensed a man's steps
behind,
His stride followed hers, to be exact.
She quickened her pace, her heart in a bind.
She prayed aloud for safety and light.
Suddenly, a ring of grace shone, bright in the
night.
The light moved with her, its presence nearby.
Did the man also see the bright light?
Her heartbeat loud, she swallowed hard.

At the fork in the road, behold he veered
away,
A wave of relief as he took his own way.
She sighed in relief, her heart filled with
praise,
She knew God was here.
With thanksgiving, she climbed the hill,
God's protection near, His love standing still.
At that moment, her soul found peace,
For in His arms, all fears would cease.
A very present help, our strength and shield,

Once My Home, Now a Memory

Once, a house stood, vast and bright,
Where memories flourished in soft, warm
light.
Antler's heads adorned the door,
An oval mirror reflected our smiles, our
space.

Through windows wide, the garden bloomed,
Mangoes, guavas and palm trees loomed.
We'd tiptoe in, with hearts in flight,
Knowing pappa's gaze would catch any slight.

The hall was filled with rays of light,
Piano notes ringing, kerosine lamps lit the
night
Pappa's office, a room calm and true,
In the garden, trees and sunlight grew.

Outside, my mother worked, we helped
Breaking leaves, gathering grass, though a
doctor.
She milked the cows, fed them and cleaned,
While hens clucked and roamed the place.
Her parrots chattered, singing with cheer,
'Good morning, How are you...' their voices
clear.

We grew up and went in different directions.
Then came the war, soldiers occupied the
home left behind.
Years went by, I went back to see,
My home, a ruin where dreams used to be.

Only the gate stood firm on the ground,
No garden, no walls, no laughter's sound.
After decades gone, what did I hope to find?
The child in me, in denial, refused to accept.

A Daughter's Return

By Lankan coast where waves endlessly play,
Lies Trincomalee, where I grew up for a time.
Famous temples and forts, the beaches so
wide,
Echoes of youth, and numerous dreams.

Mother's clinic, a milkshake every day.
A small house by the shore, where the sea
waves roar.
Distant view of ships, dark blue sea
Dad passed and was laid to rest here
Time moved us away to another land,

Through the haze of civil war and its ravages,
Years rolled by. But I returned one day.
At dawn, I ventured out;
A sense of wonder filled my heart,
As I realised, so full of gratitude,
That I had spent the night in the very place
Where my mother's clinic once stood.

Next door was the cemetery.

Somewhere within was my father's grave.
I searched through the overgrown frame,
But his grave I could not find
Disappointed and lost in thoughts
Didn't know a surprise awaited me next day.
A lady sought me with a knowing gaze,
'I knew your mother; you look so much like
her.
Also my father rests near your papa's grave.
I tend to both their graves every year'.

To a daughter far from her father's rest,
These words were music in her ears

Call these a chance, or a divine design,

Not Gods, Just Healers

We doctors come in all shapes and sizes,
Some with calm smiles, others with surprises.
Men, women or neither – one thing's the
same,
We share a purpose, not just a name.
GPs, specialists, supers and more,
Each unlocking a different health door.

Our youth? Spent buried in books,
While the girls and boys enjoy their years
We traded late nights of fun and laughter,
For endless exams, one after another.
Armed with skills and knowledge, we take on
the fight,
Decoding mysteries both day and night.

Yet diseases evolve, keeping us on our toes,
New puzzles appear wherever life flows.
We win some battles, and lose a few,
For not all outcomes are within control

But Doctors are human, flawed like others,
Navigating fears while hiding their tears.

Our judgment may falter.
What if we miss, or misinterpret the signs?
What if the answers don't fit the lines?
Experience polishes every skill.
Books, seniors and patients enrich our
knowledge.

We persist, though the cost is steep,
Sleepless nights and promises we keep.
So, before you judge, do pause and see,
A doctor's life is not burden-free.
We are not Gods, just healers.

My love for Orchids

There is something about Orchids
That I love, like no other
Elegant, and unique they speak to me softly
A mysterious and royal air about them

Such intricacy and often asymmetrical
blooms
Clothed in pristine whites, sunny yellows to
deep purples and fiery reds.
The spots, stripes or gradients, add to their
visual allure.
Their velvety soft petals so delicate, I dare to
touch
The fragrance mild appeals to my senses
Their long, slender stems, graceful blooms
smite me

At their combination of love, beauty and
strength, I marvel
Fragility with resilience, subtlety with drama
and simplicity with complexity.
Orchids aren't just flowers but wonders of
nature's artistry

Kokarako House

The Kokarako calls at dawn,
Raja struts with Ranee, restless in the coop.
Out they rush – kok ko ko kok–
Raja tall, regal, a king among birds.

His feathers trimmed, his pride intact,
His comb blazes red, hackles gleam like silk.
In the concrete maze of Chennai,
Mogappair echoes with his song.

Green Valley House is now Kokarako House,
Raja reigns, unafraid,
Scratching earth alongside Nicky, my dog.
Bold and fearless, they command the garden.

But today, audacious Raja
Marched into our hall,
Claiming new territory with Ranee in tow.

'How dare you'! I scolded,
But his gaze, sovereign and steady,
Left me chuckling despite myself.

Their stubborn charm grows on me.
Their calls carry me back to childhood,
To chickens we once had.

Perhaps, one day,
I'll let them claim my lap,
A place reserved for babies, Nicky and his
likes.

Who Killed My Red Hen?

On a calm and quiet morn, beneath the sky so
blue,
Our garden hummed with lively sounds– \
The lovebirds chirped, the rooster crowed,
The hens clucked softly by their coop.
Yet something was wrong.
The red hen, proud with eggs to guard,
Had vanished from her nest.
No feathers strewn, no blood in sight,
Her fate became a quest.

Was it a cat that stole her life?
A snake that slithered nearby?
Or could it be the watchman's hand,
The culprit I should fear?
Maybe I should hire Sherlock Holmes,
As in the garden, Nicky my dog stood,
His jaws lined with feathers,
'Ah, he ate just a crow', I told myself,
'No answer here will I uncover'.

But as the evening search went on,
A pile of feathers I found beneath the
coconut tree,
The telltale signs of my missing red hen,
The mystery is starting to unravel free.

Nicky, loyal yet treacherous,
Who stood innocent and perplexed,
Was really the killer of my dear red hen.
Oh, I am sorry, watchman,
For my suspicions dense

The brevity of Life

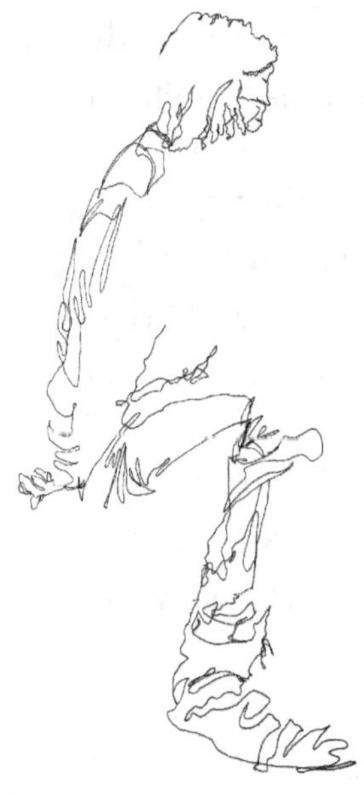

Squinting to read the paper,
His wrinkled hands tremble.
His wife – a stranger now,
A face without a name.

The beautiful house, once filled with laughter,
Echoes hollow, a weight he cannot bear.
Shields and victory cups spark fleeting
memories,
The easel, the brushes – were they his?

His juniors, now accomplished,
Gaze in silence at the lost look in his eyes.
He was the finest surgeon, they recall,
Once an orator, now a whisper.

Einstein, Pluto, the Queen,
Or the homeless man on the street–
Life, unpredictable and brief,
Slips through fingers like sand.

So, when does life truly end–
When the mind fades,
Or when the heart finally stops?